Ranger Red Presents

Blossom
The Ringtail Possum

by Bradley R Holland
Illustrated by Danny Goldsmith
and Dave Unwin

First published 2015
This edition published July 2016
Text copyright © Bradley R Holland
Illustrations copyright © Danny Capobianco and Dave Unwin
All rights reserved
Typeset by Valerie Goodreid

ISBN: 978-0-9943385-1-8

Ranger Red brings his native animals to visit groups of children. The children love to meet the animals and learn all about them.

Today, Ranger Red starts with Blossom, the Ringtail Possum.

Ranger Red says, "I need everyone to be very quiet."

He reaches into his carry box and brings out a ball of leaves.

"This is called a drey. When I gently open the lid, we can see Blossom, the Ringtail Possum."

Ranger Red shows the children how to use two fingers to gently stroke Blossom's back.

He explains, "We don't pat Blossom because she's not a pet, she's an educational native animal."

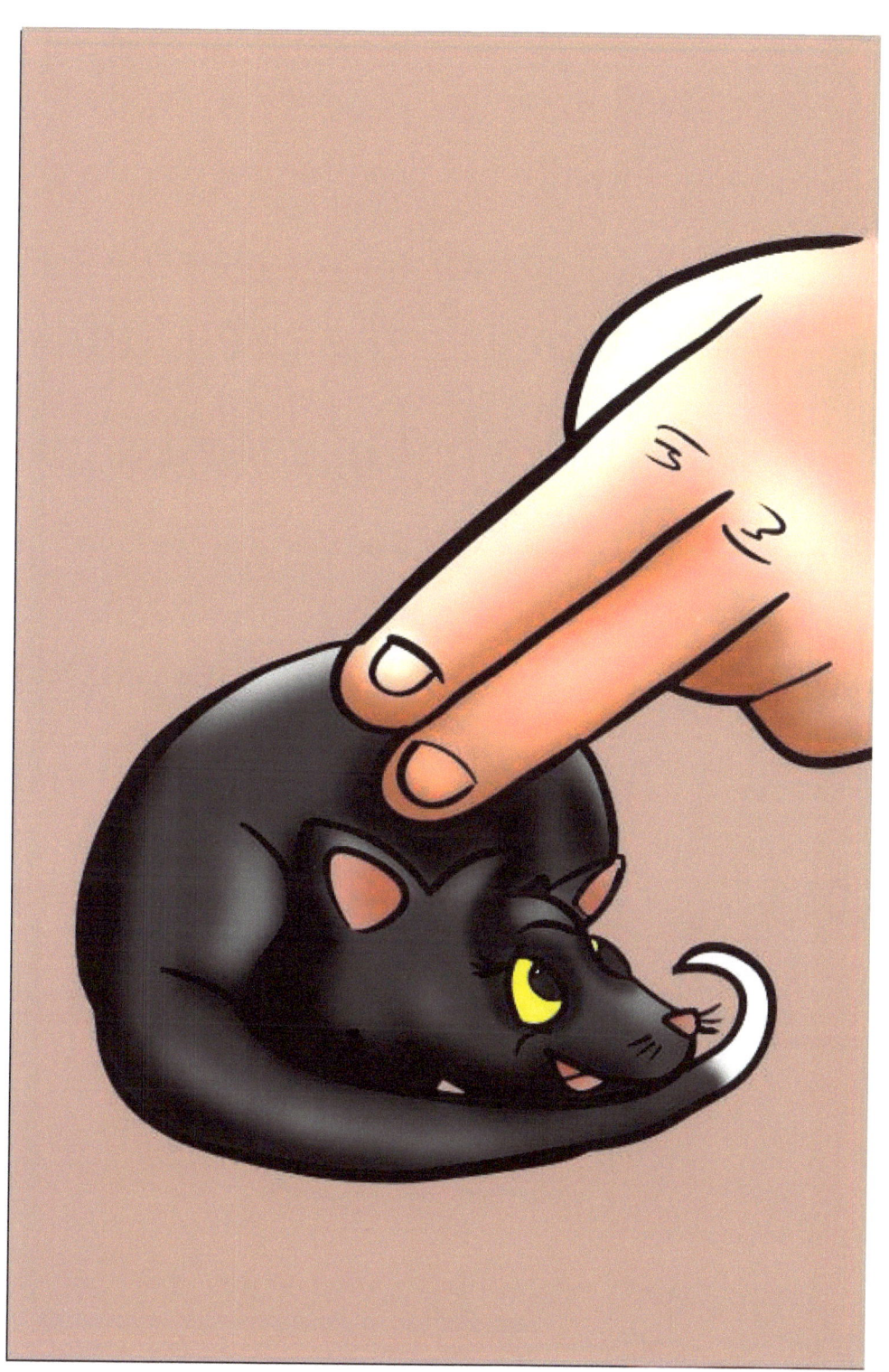

Blossom sleeps inside the drey, and so does her baby. The baby, called a joey, lives inside her pouch.

Blossom is a marsupial. Marsupials are native Australian animals with pouches for their young.

The joey stays warm and safe in Blossom's pouch for about four months, drinking milk and growing bigger. When the joey is big enough, it will ride around on Blossom's back.

Blossom gets her name from the native flowers and leaves she feeds on. Her favourite food is the Western Australian peppermint tree.

Blossom is nocturnal. She sleeps during the day and wakes up to run through the trees at night.

Blossom's tail is long and strong. She curls it around branches to help her climb through the canopy. She can support her whole body weight with her tail, and even use it to carry things.

Ranger Red explains how Blossom scratches her nose with her toes. He scratches his own nose to show the children. Then Ranger Red talks about Blossom's whiskers. They help her to feel her way through the bushes.

Finally, Ranger Red packs Blossom and her joey and their drey away in his carry box.

"But wait," says Ranger Red. "What might be in this next carry box?"

We'll just have to wait and see...

About The Author

Ranger Red has always had a unique appreciation for animals and nature. His love of native fauna was lifted to new heights with the gift of a Stimson python (Antaresia stimsoni) specimen from Harry Butler of Barrow Island when he was six years old.

Moving to Sydney at the age of eighteen, Ranger Red had the pleasure of owning his own private zoo. He held numerous jobs in Sydney: chef, toddler drama teacher, and actor performing on television, radio and theatre - to name just a few. However, his most significant and enlightening time was spent working with Anthony Stimson, owner/director of Australian Wildlife Display. While working with Anthony, Ranger Red learned the basics of running a business devoted to educating the public about our unique native wildlife. The original Blossom was a Common Ringtail possum in Anthony's display. With Anthony's encouragement, Ranger Red returned to Perth in 2009.

Red's Roving Australian Wildlife Display has been in operation since shortly after his return, bringing a hands-on native animal encounter to countless children and adults all around WA. From this grew the dream to create an educational, hands-on conservation park. Following on from his twelve book series, Ranger Red Presents, we hope to begin work in 2016 on the Ranger Red Zoo and Conservation Park, with the help of the Ranger Red Shed Association (established 2014).

About The Illustrators

Danny Capobiaco: In 2007, Danny completed a National diploma of animal care and management in England, and took these skills with him to Australia to pursue a career with wildlife. Since his move to Australia, Danny has been surrounded by Ranger Reds wildlife family and has worked with a variety of birds for over 3 years.

David Unwin was born in 1987 in Cambridgeshire England UK. He has always had a great passion for illustrating and was incredibly inspired by the wildlife Australia had to offer upon a previous visit to WA. David has put his illustration skills to great use by providing all the illustrations with their wonderful texture, editing and colour.

Western Ringtail Possum
Scientific Name: Pseudocheirus occidentalis
Noongar name: Ngwayir

The Western Ringtail Possum is a small to medium nocturnal marsupial, found exclusively in the south west of Western Australia. It has dark brown fur, with a creamy white or light grey underside. The body is usually 30-40 cm long, and the prehensile tail is as long as the body. Unlike brushtail possums, Western Ringtail possums have small, rounded ears and long thin tails.

The preferred diet of the Western Ringtail Possum is myrtaceous foliage, especially the West Australian peppermint Tree (Agonis Flexuosa). When the peppermint tree is unavailable, Western Ringtail Possums will also eat Jarrah, Marri, Wandoo, Sheok, and other native trees.

Western Ringtail Possums living in peppermint trees are most likely to build dreys. Other daytime sleeping arrangements can include hollow trees, sheltered spots in trees or occasionally on the ground, or even sleeping sitting upright in the fork of a tree.

In urban areas, Western Ringtail Possums will shelter in man-made structures, include roof spaces in houses, sheds and other buildings. They will expand their diet to include fruit trees and roses.

Western Ringtail Possums have a relatively short lifespan, usually living for three to four years. They breed once per year, usually giving birth to a single joey. Births of twins happen occasionally, with triplets happening very rarely.

Joeys live in the pouch for three to four months, and are weaned at six to eight months. Around eight to twelve months, possums will disperse, and begin breeding at twelve months.

The Western Ringtail Possum has an eastern-states cousin, the Common Ringtail Possum (Pseudocheirus peregrinus).

Endangered!

The Western Ringtail Possum was listed as vulnerable, but in December 2014 this was upgraded to endangered. Population numbers have fallen dramatically over the last ten years, and are predicted to continue falling. The main concerns for Western Ringtail Possum (as for many of our native fauna) are loss of habitat due to clearing and logging, and untimely deaths due to predation and vehicle strikes. Predators, including feral cats, foxes, and even domestic pets, are responsible for large numbers of possum deaths.

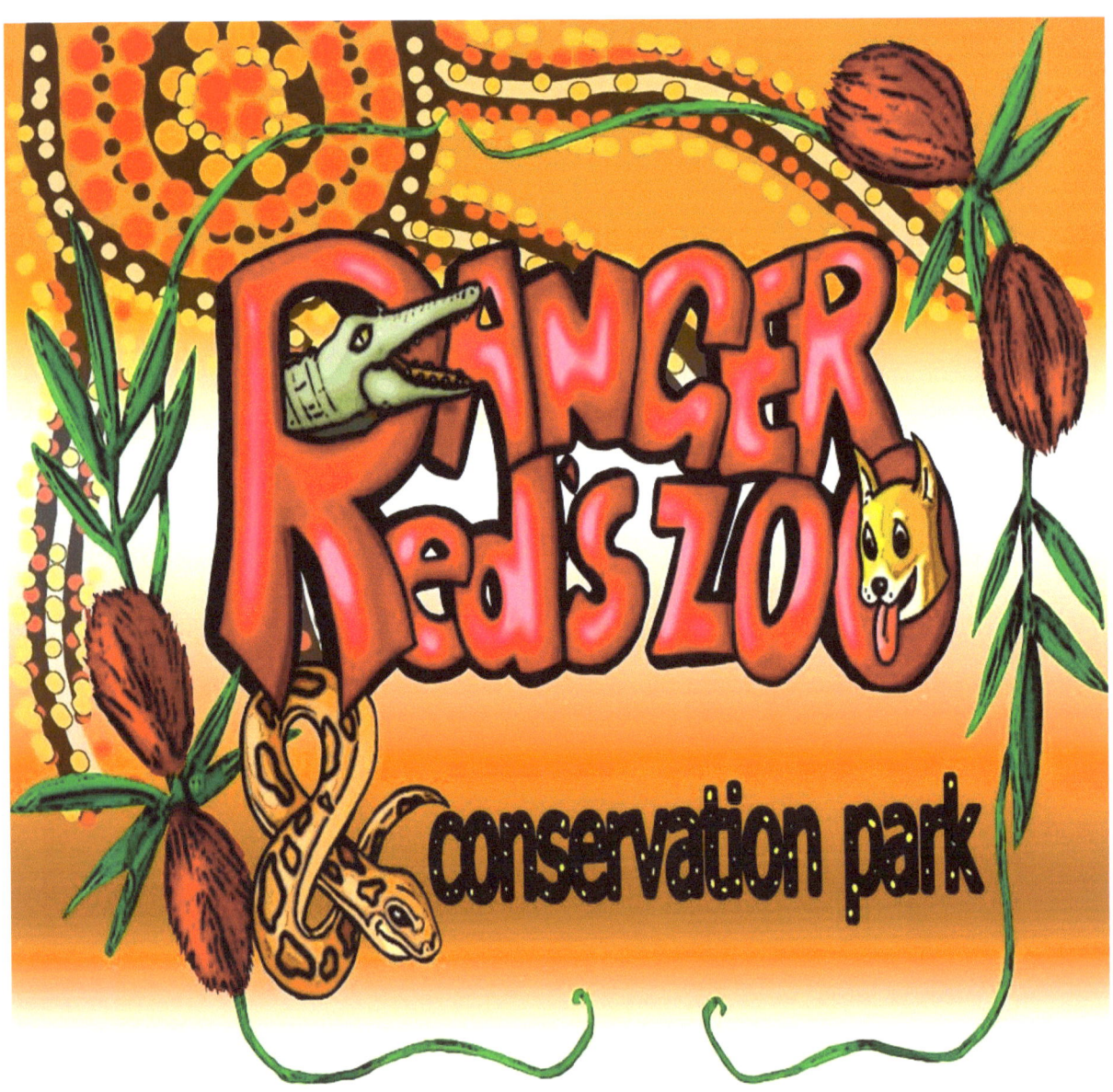

Proceeds from the sale of this book will be used to help establish Ranger Red's Zoo and Conservation Park. The vision is to develop a program that will benefit native flora and fauna, and also provide employment and purpose for both youth and older people looking for a new direction.

To find out more about how you can help, go to www.rangerred.com

www.ingramcontent.com/pod-product-compliance
Lightning Source LLC
Chambersburg PA
CBHW042129040426
42450CB00002B/130